Masters of Music
THE WORLD'S GREATEST COMPOSERS

The Life and Times of
Frédéric Chopin

D1131867

Mitchell Lane
PUBLISHERS

P.O. Box 196
Hockessin, Delaware 19707

Masters of Music
THE WORLD'S GREATEST COMPOSERS

Titles in the Series
The Life and Times of...

Visit us on the web: www.mitchelllane.com
Comments? email us: mitchelllane@mitchelllane.com

Masters of Music
THE WORLD'S GREATEST COMPOSERS

The Life and Times of
Frédéric Chopin

by Jim Whiting

Mitchell Lane
PUBLISHERS

Printing   1   2   3   4   5   6   7   8
        Library of Congress Cataloging-in-Publication Data
Whiting, Jim, 1943-
        The Life and Times of Frédéric Chopin/Jim Whiting.
            p. cm. — (Masters of Music. World's greatest composers)
        Contents: The patriotic pianist—Growing up happy—On to Paris—George Sand—Alone
        Includes bibliographical references (p.) and index.
            ISBN 1-58415-245-1 (lib bdg.)
        1. Chopin, Frédéric, 1810-1849—Juvenile literature. 2. Composers—Biography—Juvenile
        literature. [1. Chopin, Frédéric, 1810-1849. 2. Composers.] I. Title. II. Series.
        ML3930.C46 W43 2004
        786.2'092—dc22   2003024048

ABOUT THE AUTHOR: Jim Whiting has been a journalist, writer, editor, and photographer for more than 20 years. In addition to a lengthy stint as publisher of *Northwest Runner* magazine, Mr. Whiting has contributed articles to the *Seattle Times*, *Conde Nast Traveler*, *Newsday*, and *Saturday Evening Post*. He has edited more than 20 titles in the Mitchell Lane Real-Life Reader Biography series and Unlocking the Secrets of Science. He lives in Washington state with his wife and two teenage sons.

PHOTO CREDITS: Cover: PhotoResearchers; p. 6 PhotoSource; p. 10 (left and right) PhotoSource; p. 11 Corbis; p. 12 Hulton/Archive; p. 14 Chopin Institute; p. 16 Corbis; pp. 20, 23, 24, 28, 36 Hulton/Archive

PUBLISHER'S NOTE: This story is based on the author's extensive research, which he believes to be accurate. Documentation of such research is contained on pages 46-47.

The internet sites referenced herein were active as of the publication date. Due to the fleeting nature of some web sites, we cannot guarantee they will all be active when you are reading this book.

Contents

The Life and Times of
Frédéric Chopin

by Jim Whiting

* For Your Information

Adrien Brody portrays Wladyslaw Szpilman in the movie "The Pianist." Szpilman was a 27-year-old pianist, who played the classics on Polish radio in Warsaw when the Nazis invaded Poland in 1939. Much of the music in "The Pianist" was written by Frédéric Chopin.

The Patriotic Pianist

On the night of August 31, 1939, many Germans were listening to a broadcast of music on their radios. The transmitter was in the town of Gleiwitz, located on the border with Poland. Suddenly the music stopped. The excited announcer came on the air to say that Polish troops were closing in on the radio station. Then the sound went dead.

Minutes later, broadcasting resumed. Only it wasn't the German announcer. Strange voices shouted anti-German slogans in Polish. Listeners heard shots being fired. Again the sound went dead.

The following morning, German dictator Adolf Hitler gave a speech. "This night for the first time Polish regular soldiers fired on our own territory," he said. "Since 5:45 A.M. we have been returning the fire, and from now on bombs will be met with bombs."[1]

Hitler's words "returning the fire" were a huge understatement. The German army had launched a massive invasion of Poland, using the attack on the radio station as their reason. But Hitler was lying. No "Polish regular soldiers" had invaded German territory. The anti-German slogans that shocked listeners had been shouted by Polish-speaking German soldiers. When foreign newspapermen were taken to Gleiwitz, they saw several dead bodies in Polish army uniforms. But the dead men weren't soldiers. They were inmates from a German concentration camp. They had been given injections the previous day to make them unconscious. Then they were dressed in the uniforms. While still unconscious, they were shot. Then their bodies were arranged to make it appear that they had been killed by German police in the struggle for the station.

Hitler had been planning to invade Poland for months. He had already taken over Austria and Czechoslovakia without having to fire any shots. He knew that Poland would be different. It had a large army and wouldn't willingly surrender. Acting on his orders, nearly two million German soldiers and airmen took up positions along the border with Poland during the summer. Even though there was no doubt in his mind that he would launch an invasion, Hitler felt he somehow needed a justification. The fake raid provided one.

Even though the Germans had many more heavy tanks than the Poles, and although German warplanes controlled the skies, Polish troops fought back bravely. They even managed to slow down the German advance. But on September 17, a huge army from the Soviet Union invaded Poland from the other side. The country was doomed.

Several days later, German troops arrived at the outskirts of Warsaw, Poland's capital city. They began a bombardment with heavy artillery. Some of the shells fell near the Polish National Radio station in the heart of the city. Inside the building, a young pianist named Wladyslaw Szpilman was playing music by Frédéric Chopin (pronounced show-PAN). The piece was Nocturne in C-sharp Minor. Szpilman's choice of music was symbolic. Chopin was a national hero in Poland, and his music represented freedom and independence. Szpilman's playing proved to be one of Poland's final acts of defiance. Before he could finish, artillery shells hit the station and forced it off the air.

This incident, symbolizing the end of Poland's independence in the early days of World War II, marks the beginning of the highly acclaimed 2002 film *The Pianist*. The movie is based on the book that Szpilman wrote about his experiences. Szpilman was Jewish, and millions of his fellow Jews were herded into German concentration camps, where nearly all of them were gassed. Szpilman escaped this fate, a number of times by the narrowest of margins. Chopin's music runs throughout the film, and it probably saves Szpilman's life. As he scrounges for food in an abandoned house near the end of the movie, he is discovered by a German officer.

Under most circumstances that would have meant certain death. The officer would simply have turned him in, and Szpilman quickly would have been on his way to one of the concentration camps. Fortunately for Szpilman, the officer asks him what he does. Szpilman replies that he is a pianist. There is a piano in the house, and the officer asks Szpilman to play some music for him. Because of the necessity for utter silence while he was hiding, it is the first time in years that Szpilman has been able to play. He has whiled away the long, lonely hours by rehearsing Chopin's music in his imagination. Now that he finally has the chance to sit in front of a real piano, Szpilman makes the most of his opportunity. His wonderful playing impresses the German officer, who not only allows Szpilman to live but also helps him to survive by secretly bringing him food. When the Germans finally evacuate Warsaw in early 1945, the officer even gives Szpilman a heavy overcoat to help him keep warm.

The Pianist concludes with a highly symbolic scene. The Polish state radio goes back on the air after the Germans are defeated. Its first broadcast is Szpilman once again playing Chopin's Nocturne in C-sharp Minor. This time there are no interruptions.

Adrien Brody won an Academy Award, or Oscar, for Best Actor for his portrayal of Szpilman, while Roman Polanski received an Oscar for Best Director. Polanski had firsthand experience of the types of struggles and dangers that Szpilman went through. As a boy in Poland during World War II, he narrowly escaped being sent to a concentration camp himself. He has said, "For us Poles, Chopin symbolizes revolution. It is not surprising that his monument in Warsaw was pulled down during World War II, nor that the wartime struggles led to his music being banned in Poland. His music is our music—it's like mother's milk. It is what gave Szpilman strength and courage."[2] ◆

Wladyslaw Szpilman, shown here in 2002 (left) and on the cover of one of his recordings, right, escaped the horrors of Adolf Hitler's reign of terror and lived to tell about it. Chopin is one of his favorite composers.

Lech Walesa

A Brief History of Poland

Poland as a country dates back to the tenth century. Over the next few centuries its territory gradually increased. By the end of the sixteenth century, Poland had achieved its maximum political power; it was also influential culturally and intellectually. For example, famous astronomer Nicolaus Copernicus, who proved that Earth revolves around the sun, was Polish.

But wars, internal conflicts, and powerful neighbors began to weaken the country. In a series of three partitions between 1772 and 1795 among Russia, Austria, and Prussia, Poland disappeared from the map of Europe. Under the reign of Russian Czar Alexander I, a small Polish kingdom was allowed to exist during the early years of the nineteenth century, but it was under strict Russian control. Polish national pride wasn't easy to overcome, however, and there were several uprisings that tried to restore its independence. One of them came in 1830, shortly after Chopin had left his native land for good. The uprising didn't succeed.

After the end of World War I, an independent Polish state was created. Part of its territory had belonged to Germany before the war. When German dictator Adolf Hitler came to power in 1933, he wanted to reclaim that land. Six years later, he launched his invasion. Less than three weeks after the Germans poured into Poland from the west side, a huge army from the Soviet Union (Russia and 15 other republics) crossed Poland's eastern border. Again Poland disappeared as its territory was divided between its two conquerors. By that time, many Jews were living in Poland. Several million were taken to German concentration camps and killed in the gas chambers.

With the German defeat in 1945, the nation of Poland was again created. It quickly came under the Polish Communist Party, which in turn was controlled by the Soviet Union. Increasing unrest during the next several decades resulted in the formation of the Solidarity labor movement in 1980 under the leadership of a shipyard worker named Lech Walesa. Elections were held in 1990 after the collapse of the Soviet Union. Walesa was elected as the country's president. Poland was finally free.

Frédéric Chopin as a young man. Even at an early age, it was obvious that he possessed unusual musical talent. Though he left Poland when he was 20 and never returned, he always carried a small urn that contained Polish soil.

Growing Up Happy

F rédéric François Chopin (his first name sometimes appears as Fryderyk, the original Polish spelling, but he is far better known as Frédéric) was born on March 1, 1810, in the village of Zelazowa Wola, Poland. His parents were Justyna and Nicholas Chopin. Nicholas Chopin, born in France, moved to Poland by himself when he was just seventeen. At first he got a job as a bookkeeper in a factory in Warsaw, Poland's largest city. Nicholas was an intelligent young man who eventually became a tutor for the Skarbecks. They were a noble family who lived just outside Warsaw in Zelazowa Wola. He quickly became acquainted with Justyna Krzyzanowska, who was probably a poor relation of the Skarbecks and acted as their housekeeper. The couple was married four years after Nicholas arrived.

Frédéric was the couple's second child and only son. His older sister Ludwika (or Louise, as she is more commonly known) had been born almost three years earlier. Two more girls, Isabella and Emilia, were born soon afterward.

When Frédéric was five, the family moved to Warsaw. Nicholas had taken a job at the Warsaw Lyceum. Soon he became so successful that he started his own school. Frédéric grew up in a peaceful, cultured household. The children learned to speak both Polish and French. Their home contained a large library. The family regularly played music together. Often the children would travel to the nearby woods with their father, where they would hunt for strawberries and mushrooms.

Everyone looked forward to Christmas. As authors George Marek and Maria Gordon-Smith explain, "It was a fast day: one did not eat until the first star rose (about 6 P.M.), symbol of the star which heralded the birth of the baby in the manger. . . . The table was covered with the best tablecloth, underneath which a thin layer of hay had been spread, denoting the successful completion of the harvest as well as the Infant's crib. Dinner began. And what a

House in Zelazowa Wola where Chopin was born. His birthplace is still standing, today a museum dedicated to his memory. In Chopin's day, the house belonged to the Skarbek family, who employed Chopin's father, Nicholas, as a tutor for their children.

dinner! Twelve or thirteen courses, all traditional."[1] Afterward everyone would exchange gifts and sing Christmas songs.

By nearly all accounts, therefore, Frédéric enjoyed a happy childhood. His mother gave piano lessons to her children, and it soon became apparent that Frédéric had a great deal of natural ability. By the time he turned six, he had absorbed all that she had to teach. The family hired Wojciech (or Albert) Zwyny, a 60-year-old who claimed that he had studied with a pupil of the great Johann Sebastian Bach.

Zwyny proved to be a good teacher. He gave young Frédéric a grounding in piano technique. Just as important, he encouraged him to improvise and write down what he had just played. When he was seven, Frédéric composed his first work, which he called Polonaise for Piano-Forte. He gave a brief public performance one week before his eighth birthday. Zwyny sensed that he had something special in the youngster. He would often ignore his other pupils to give Frédéric extra attention.

The local papers were quick to take notice. One called Frédéric a "true musical genius" and noted, "Not only does he play the most difficult piano pieces with the greatest ease and the most extraordinary taste, he is already the composer of several dances and variations, each of which has thoroughly astonished the connoisseurs, especially in view of his tender age."[2]

This "tender age" naturally drew comparisons with Wolfgang Mozart, who had exhibited similar accomplishments at a young age several decades earlier. Like Mozart, Frédéric was invited to play for members of the aristocracy in small private concerts. Unlike Mozart, however, his parents didn't take advantage of his youth. There were too many stories of young prodigies who were quickly forgotten.

Wolfgang Amadeus Mozart was a genuine child prodigy. He learned to play the piano when he was very young. He took his first public concert tour when he was only six, playing before kings and packed houses. He also began composing at about that time. Tragically, he died when he was only 35.

"His father was too wise to let it happen," Marek and Gordon-Smith write. "Frédéric was allowed to build his talent quietly, nourished by the impressions made on him by the open countryside, youthful friendships, books and talk."[3] It would be five years before he would make another public concert appearance.

Before that happened, in 1822, Zwyny realized that he had taught his young charge all that he had to offer. The previous year, a man named Jósef Elsner had established a new music school in Warsaw. Though his music isn't played today, Elsner was a very prolific composer and had written virtually every type of music. It was decided that Frédéric would attend Elsner's school. A violinist himself, Elsner taught the boy more about music theory and composition than piano technique. That allowed Frédéric to continue to develop his own unique style.

Elsner wrote about his prize pupil: "Leave him in peace. If his method is out of the ordinary, so is his talent. What need has he of adhering rigorously to the usual rules? He follows rules of his own."[4]

So when Frédéric gave his second concert early in 1823 at the age of 13, the newspaper reviews were just as complimentary as the first ones.

Frédéric didn't let this praise go to his head. At school, he fit in well with the other students. Once he drew a very unflattering caricature of one of the teachers and passed it around. The teacher saw it. He was humorous enough to return it to the artist and mark it "well drawn."

Josephine Wodzinska, the older sister of a young woman to whom Frédéric would eventually become engaged, remembered the early days fondly. "When we visited the Chopins all we had in mind was playing games," she wrote. "That Frédéric was already considered the best pianist in Warsaw didn't mean nearly as much to us as that he was ready for jokes and fun . . . running, clowning, imitating people we knew—he did that best—sketching. . . . Sometimes he would sit at the piano, but because we were too young to take music seriously, he would play tricks or play dance tunes."[5]

Frédéric entered the Warsaw Conservatory in 1826. His sister Emilia died of tuberculosis the following year at the age of 14. At that time, tuberculosis was a common disease, and there was little that doctors could do for those who caught it. The disease had no cure and was frequently fatal. By then, Frédéric had had several serious illnesses himself, indications of the ill health that would plague him for much of his life.

Despite his sorrow, Frédéric composed a set of variations on the aria "La ci darem la mano" from Mozart's opera *Don Giovanni*. It created a sensation when it was published in 1830. When he heard it, composer Robert Schumann wrote, "Hats off, gentlemen—a genius!"[6]

In the summer of 1828 Frédéric traveled to Berlin with a friend of his father's. It was his first big trip. He saw several famous composers, such as Felix Mendelssohn. But he was too shy to introduce himself to them. By the time he graduated from the conservatory the following year, it seemed evident that he needed to leave Warsaw to advance his career.

He made a short visit to Vienna. Despite his shyness, he played as part of a public concert. He was amazed when the audience rose to its feet to cheer him. The newspaper reviews were positive, though there was one small reservation. His playing seemed to be too subdued to some people. It didn't matter now. It would matter much more in the future.

He returned home after several weeks, but the glimpses of what might be possible were irresistible. He quickly became restless. Warsaw was too far off the artistic beaten track for someone to make a serious reputation.

There was little doubt that he was ready to spread his artistic wings. Elsner's final three annual evaluations of Chopin's talent simply added official confirmation:

1827: "Exceptionally gifted."[7]

1828: "Extraordinarily endowed."[8]

1829: "Extraordinarily endowed. A musical genius."[9]

In 1830 Frédéric spent most of the month of October preparing for the journey to Vienna. On the morning of November 2, the stagecoach stopped at Zelazowa Wola to pick up the young man. His teacher, Elsner, led a choir in singing a cantata that Elsner had composed in honor of the special occasion. Frédéric embraced his family, then climbed into the coach.

He didn't know it at the time, but he would never return to Poland. ◆

Miguel Hidalgo

MEXICO'S "FOURTH OF JULY"

The year 1810 saw another birth besides Chopin's. Mexican independence was also born that year. While many people believe that Cinco de Mayo (May 5) is the Mexican equivalent of the Fourth of July, Mexico actually celebrates its independence on September 16. On that date in 1810 in the village of Dolores, a Catholic priest named Miguel Hidalgo y Costilla gathered his parishioners, who were mostly American Indians and mestizos (persons of mixed Indian and Spanish heritage). In a passionate speech known as "El Grito de Dolores" (The Cry of Sorrows), Hidalgo urged them to rise up against their Spanish oppressors. The Indians, who had lost their native land to the invading Spanish nearly 300 years earlier, went on a rampage, butchering as many Spanish as they could find. Then they marched toward the capital, Mexico City, but couldn't capture it.

The following year, Hidalgo himself was captured. He was executed by a firing squad. His head was cut off and displayed as a warning. While other rebel leaders continued the fight, by 1820 the movement toward independence had almost been extinguished. Then an officer named Agustín de Iturbide, who was originally loyal to Spain, switched his allegiance to the rebels. At the head of the victorious army, he entered Mexico City in September 1821. Mexico was free.

At exactly 11:00 P.M. on September 15 every year, the Mexican president appears on the National Palace's main balcony and repeats "El Grito." Fireworks flash in the night sky as he finishes. Parades and fiestas are held throughout the country the following day.

What is Cinco de Mayo? On May 5, 1862, an outnumbered, ill-equipped Mexican army defeated invading French troops at the Battle of Puebla. Though a much larger French army would eventually invade Mexico and establish the short reign of Emperor Maximilian, the earlier Mexican victory has continued to be a source of national pride.

French composer Hector Berlioz became one of Chopin's friends soon after he arrived in Paris. Berlioz was especially famous for his imaginative orchestrations. These included a lively version of "La Marseillaise," the French national anthem.

On to Paris

W ith bad roads and several stops, it took Chopin three weeks to arrive in Vienna. He quickly found lodgings. Within a week, however, he heard disturbing news. A revolt back in Warsaw had broken out against the Russians. He was afraid for the safety of his family.

His mind wasn't set at ease either by what was happening to him personally. Fashions in piano playing had changed during the few months since his previous visit. Now the Viennese public wanted pianists who would dazzle them with the exuberant quality of their playing. Chopin's somewhat subdued style wasn't very appealing. No one was interested in putting on a concert that would feature him. Nor did he do any better in trying to have his music published.

Even though he attended a number of parties, he was still lonely. It was hard not to feel that he was wasting his parents' money. His doubts increased when he finally organized two concerts for the following spring and neither one was successful.

By then it seemed obvious that he would have a difficult time in Vienna. He decided to move to Paris, the capital and largest city of France. During a stopover in Stuttgart, Germany, Chopin received the horrifying news that the revolt in Poland had been crushed. He was still worried about his family's safety, but there was nothing he could do. He finally arrived in Paris in mid-September 1831.

It had been just over a year since a revolution had installed King Louis-Philippe in power. The new king was considered more open to freedom and democratic principles than his predecessor had been. Reflecting the optimistic mood, a new arrangement of the inspiring French national anthem "La Marseillaise" had recently been published by the young composer Hector Berlioz. It was common for people to sing its rousing melody on the streets. Chopin was also heartened because thousands of exiles from Poland were there.

In a letter to a Polish friend, Norbert Alfons Kumelski, Chopin was enthusiastic about his new home. "I reached Paris quite safely although it cost me a lot, and I am delighted with what I have found," he wrote. "I have the finest musicians and opera in the world."[1]

In a political climate that stressed the importance of freedom—totally different from what Chopin would have faced if he were still in Warsaw—the arts were thriving. Whether it was literature, painting, orchestral music, opera, even piano manufacturing, Paris was the cultural center of Europe. Chopin quickly met many important artists. These included composers such as Berlioz, Mendelssohn, Gioacchino Rossini, Luigi Cherubini, and Franz Liszt. Another friend was a painter, Eugène Delacroix.

In his enthusiasm, young Frédéric almost made a big mistake right away. He became acquainted with Friedrich Kalkbrenner, one of the most famous pianists in the city. Even though his style of playing was very different from Chopin's, the new arrival was impressed.

Felix Mendelssohn was another of Chopin's friends. A distinguished composer and conductor, Mendelssohn is credited with helping to restore interest in the music of Johann Sebastian Bach after it had been virtually ignored for many years. Like several other famous composers, Mendelssohn didn't live very long, dying at the age of 38.

"It is hard to describe his calm, enchanting touch, his incomparable evenness,"[2] he wrote about Kalkbrenner to a friend.

Kalkbrenner, a somewhat conceited man, told Chopin that he would make a great pianist of him. There was one condition: Chopin had to agree to a three-year contract. For some reason, Chopin seriously considered this offer even though he was already so successful. His father, his sister Louise, and his former teacher Elsner were horrified. They wrote him urgent letters advising against such an action.

When Chopin appeared uncertain, Kalkbrenner proposed a compromise. He was smart enough to realize that having Chopin as a pupil would reflect favorably on him. But Chopin's new friend Franz Liszt and another famous Paris pianist, Ferdinand Hiller, convinced Chopin that he was already better than Kalkbrenner.

With that brief professional flirtation behind him, Chopin gave his first public French concert in February 1832. Many famous musicians and composers were in the audience, and the concert was well received. But Chopin didn't make much money.

Early in 1833, Chopin had a stroke of good luck. He met a nobleman named Prince Valentin Radziwill, who invited him to a soiree given by a rich man named Baron James de Rothschild. The baron's wife asked Chopin to play the piano, and he became an instant hit. Many of the women in attendance, including the baron's wife, asked Chopin to give them lessons.

Just as important, he was accepted on almost an equal footing in high society. That helped to give him a reliable source of income. Many wealthy Parisians had large rooms called salons where they held recitals. Chopin was often hired to play. Since these salons held no more than a few dozen people, they were much more suited than large concert halls to Chopin's intimate style of playing.

This picture of German pianist and composer Franz Liszt dates from his later years. As a young man, he had an eight-year concert career in which he received the same adulation and enthusiasm that rock stars enjoy today.

Now that he was financially secure, he had more time for composition. That in turn led to even more money as more and more of his works became published. The most important of these were his *Twelve Grand Études,* or studies, for the piano. Published in 1833, they established his reputation as a composer.

For the next few years, Chopin lived a fairly settled life. He made a few trips outside of Paris, mostly to Germany. He spent some time with Mendelssohn, then met Robert Schumann, who had praised him three years earlier. He especially enjoyed meeting Schumann's wife, Clara, a famous pianist. He referred to her as "the only woman in Germany who can play my music."[3]

By 1835, Chopin was firmly established in his adopted city of Paris. But he still missed Poland, and especially his parents. He arranged a meeting in August that year in the German city of Karlsbad. It was a joyous reunion, as they hadn't seen each other for nearly five years.

Soon afterward, Chopin traveled to the German city of Dresden. He wanted to see the Wodzinska family, friends from his earlier days in Warsaw. He found that their daughter, Maria, was now 16. She had become a beautiful young pianist and Chopin quickly fell in love with her. But there was a problem. Maria's parents were concerned about Chopin's health, which had never been good. Even in his early 20s, he would sometimes cough up blood. When he asked their permission to marry Maria, they agreed—under one condition. He had to remain in good health. Unfortunately, he became seriously ill with the flu several months later. Eventually the wedding was called off.

Naturally, this depressed Chopin. He put all the letters he had received from Maria into a bundle and scrawled "My misery" on it. Then he sent it to her.

In the meantime he had met another woman. She would change his entire life.

Clara Schumann

Clara Schumann is generally considered to be the finest female pianist of the nineteenth century. She was born in Leipzig, Germany, on September 13, 1819. Her father, Friedrich Wieck (Veek), was a music teacher, and her mother, Marianne Wieck, was a singer.

Josef Joachim accompanied by Clara Schumann

Her father wanted her to become a child prodigy. Clara began taking piano lessons at the age of five and had her first public appearance four years later. She went on an extended tour in 1831 when she was not yet 12. She also began to compose.

At about that time, a young man named Robert Schumann moved into the Wieck home to study piano and composition with Clara's father. A few years later, when Robert was 25 and Clara was 16, they fell in love.

Friedrich didn't approve. He ordered Robert out of the house. Clara and Robert didn't see each other for more than a year. Then they reestablished contact. Robert wanted to marry Clara. Her father still refused. The young couple went to court and were granted permission. They were married when Robert was 30 and Clara was a day short of 21.

Even though both of them continued to compose music, it was virtually impossible for a woman to have her compositions played. "I once believed that I possessed creative talent, but I have given up this idea; a woman must not desire to compose,"[4] she wrote in her diary.

Clara contented herself with playing her husband's music. The couple also had eight children (one died in infancy), so Clara was kept busy raising them.

Unfortunately, Robert eventually began showing signs of mental illness. In 1854, he tried to kill himself and was committed to a mental asylum. He died there in 1856.

Clara began a series of concert tours to provide money for the family to live on, making more than 30 trips outside of Germany. She never remarried, and died in Frankfurt, Germany, on May 20, 1896.

This is a picture of George Sand, whose real name was Aurore Dudevant. She wrote a number of famous novels under her pen name. She had a ten-year relationship with Chopin, during which he wrote most of his greatest works.

George Sand

In 1836, Aurore Dudevant, a famous novelist, was 32, six years older than Chopin. Since it was much more difficult for women in that era to have their novels published than it was for men, Aurore adopted the pen name of George Sand. Even today, she is much better know by her nom de plume than her real name.

She also adopted many characteristics that are often associated with men, even more so nearly 200 years ago. She wore masculine clothing such as suits and pants, smoked cigars, and had a series of love affairs. She had married while still a teenager and had two children, Maurice (who was thirteen when his mother met Chopin) and Solange (who was eight).

Aurore came from an unusual background. Her father was descended from royalty, while her mother had not. When Aurore was just eighteen, she married Baron Casimir Dudevant. Soon afterward, she inherited her grandmother's estate in Nohant, which is located about 180 miles south of Paris. She had been raised there, spending a lot of her time outdoors riding horses and hunting wild game in the forests that surrounded the house. She often dressed in men's clothing because it was much less confining in these active pursuits. Nohant would eventually become important in Chopin's life as well.

By the time Solange was born, it was obvious that Aurore's marriage was a failure. She became involved with a young man named Jules Sandeau. Together they wrote a novel under the name of J. Sand. Then Aurore wrote another one on her own. She couldn't use either her original family name of Dupin or that of her former husband. Since she had already published one book under the name of Sand, it made sense to keep it for this new book. No one is sure why she adopted George as her new literary first name.

Her novels created a sensation. She quickly became famous and knew just about everybody in Paris who was important. The main exception was Chopin, so she wanted to meet him as well. She was a friend of Countess Marie d'Agoult, who was romantically in-volved with Franz Liszt. Through the countess, Sand asked Liszt to bring her together with Chopin. Liszt arranged a meeting that occurred sometime during the fall of 1836. It wasn't a case of "love at first sight." Chopin wasn't very impressed with her. He even asked his friend Hiller if she was really a woman. Besides, he was still in love with Maria Wodzinska.

Early in 1837, Sand invited Chopin to visit her at Nohant, but he turned down the offer. That summer, his engagement with Maria finally came to an end. So when Sand returned to Paris for a few weeks in the fall, Chopin's attitude was completely different. He saw her in an entirely new light.

"I was overcome," he wrote in his journal. "My heart was con-quered. . . . She understood me. . . . She loves me."[1]

This time it was Sand's turn to back away. She was involved with a young playwright named Felicien Mallefille, who lived with her at Nohant and served as her children's tutor. She went back home.

By the following spring she had made up her mind. It was Chopin she wanted, not a struggling playwright. She returned to Paris, determined to establish a relationship with the composer. She was mystified that he treated her coldly. None of the passion that he had shown her the previous fall was in evidence. For a while she thought that he was still in love with Maria, but soon she figured out the truth. Chopin was a shy man around women. It was difficult for him to become close on a personal level. Though he had been engaged to Maria, they had actually spent very little time together because their homes were widely separated. Once Sand realized why he seemed relatively remote, she pushed even harder. Soon they were in a romantic relationship.

Their relationship created a problem. Mallefille didn't like being rejected. As author Adam Zamoyski explains, "Mallefille was wandering around Paris uttering wild threats, and the two lovers had to be careful."[2] In addition, Sand's son, Maurice, was ill. They decided to travel to the island of Majorca, in the Mediterranean off the coast of Spain, where they expected to find both safety from Mallefille and a more congenial climate for Maurice. George and her children left Paris shortly before Chopin, then the four were reunited at the French coast. Sand wrote that her Chopin appeared "fresh as a rose, and rosy as a turnip."[3]

It wouldn't take him long to wilt.

When they arrived at Majorca a few days later, Chopin wrote enthusiastically to a friend, "I am in Palma [the island's capital city], amid palms, cedars, cacti, olives, pomegranates, etc. A sky like turquoise, a sea like lapis lazuli, mountains like emerald, air like heaven. Sun all day and hot; everyone in summer clothing; at night, guitars and singing for hours."[4]

Within a few days of their arrival, a series of heavy rainstorms began. The thick plaster walls of their house made it very cold.

They had to keep a fire burning constantly for warmth. There was no chimney, so the smoke collected inside. That would have been hard enough on Chopin's already delicate lungs. Even worse, just before the rains began, everyone had gone for a long walk, which exhausted Chopin and gave him a case of bronchitis.

It didn't take long for the disease to worsen. Chopin sent a note to a friend: "The three most celebrated doctors on the island have seen me. One sniffed at what I spat, the second tapped at what I spat, and third sounded me and listened as I spat. The first said I was dead, the second that I am dying, the third that I'm going to die."[5]

There were other unpleasantries. The island residents were pious Catholics who resented the fact that Sand and Chopin weren't married. They were also terrified of his illness because of the danger that he might pass it along to them. Not surprisingly, Chopin realized that they had made a mistake and couldn't wait to leave Majorca. Still, the weather made it too difficult and dangerous to cross back to the mainland. Finally the sea conditions improved, but the rough cart that carried Chopin to the ship jostled him so much that his lungs hemorrhaged. He nearly bled to death before arriving at the port of Marseilles in late February.

Two months later he was well enough to travel to Nohant with Sand and the children. He enjoyed living there and wrote several compositions. Then in October they all returned to Paris. They occupied two houses that were close to each other. A year and a half later they returned to Nohant. That began a pattern that continued for several years. They would spend part of the year in Paris, part in Nohant.

During those years, George Sand supplied Chopin with a great deal of tender loving care. She also supplied him with a great deal of inspiration. Sand described Chopin's working method in these words: "[Inspiration] came on his piano suddenly, complete, sublime, or it sang in his head during a walk. . . . But then began the most heart rending labor I ever saw. It was a series of efforts, of irresolutions, and of frettings to seize again certain details of the theme he had heard. . . . His regret at not finding it again . . . threw him into a kind of despair. He shut himself up for whole days, weeping, walking, breaking his pens, repeating and altering a bar a hundred times, ... and recommencing the next with a minute and desperate perseverance. He spent six weeks over a single page to write it at last as he had noted it down at the very first."[6]

This constant reworking kept him from publishing much music, and even then almost all of his completed compositions were relatively short. In 1842, for example, his Polonaise in A-flat Major—one of his most commonly performed works today—was among just five pieces he completed that year. In 1844, his only published work was his considerably longer Sonata in B Minor.

Chopin's father died that same year, and Chopin was grief-stricken. His already frail health became even worse. His sister was so concerned that she made the long trip from Warsaw to see him.

In 1846, George Sand made plans to spend an entire year in Nohant in hopes that the warmer climate would help Chopin get rid of his cough. But those plans soon fell apart. Not long afterward, their relationship did too.

One stumbling block was Chopin's relationship with Sand's children. Chopin was very close to Solange, who had developed the headstrong personality of her mother. George had problems controlling Solange's behavior and may have been jealous of the close bond that she had with Chopin. On the other hand, Chopin didn't get along with Maurice, who was now a young man. Sand often took her son's side in their disputes.

By this time, Sand was probably growing tired of taking care of Chopin. She even wrote a novel called *Lucrezia Floriani*, in which the heroine falls in love with a nobleman who is ill. In the end, the heroine dies because of the strain that the sick man has imposed on her. Except for the outcome, it was a thinly disguised version of her relationship with Chopin.

The final straw came in 1847. Solange was engaged to a respectable neighbor in Nohant. She abruptly broke off her engagement and married a sculptor named Auguste Clésinger. Chopin wasn't invited. While Sand initially approved, she and Solange began quarreling. Solange accused her mother of having a love affair with one of Maurice's friends. There was a violent scene in which Clésinger struck Sand and in turn was nearly shot by Maurice.

Solange quickly wrote to Chopin, giving him a very one-sided version of what had happened. She asked him to send a carriage so that she and her husband could get away. Not realizing the full story, Chopin agreed.

Sand was furious. She sent an angry letter to Chopin, criticizing him for sending the carriage and adding that she had forbidden Solange to ever stay with her again. In essence, she was asking Chopin to choose between her and her daughter. He took several days to answer, then replied calmly that he refused to make any such decision. That was it. After being together for nearly a decade, George Sand and Frédéric Chopin parted in anger and bitterness.

"After the break they met once, by accident," according to author Harold C. Schonberg. "Chopin was leaving a party, Sand entering. They had a few words in front of the door. 'She asked me how I was,' Chopin wrote to Solange. 'I said I was well, and then I called for the concierge to open the door. I raised my hat and walked home to the Square d'Orléans.' With these banalities they parted forever."[7]

Women Take Pen Names

George Eliot

George Sand wasn't the only nineteenth-century woman writer who used a man's pen name to give herself a better chance of being published. Mary Ann Evans wrote such novels as *Middlemarch, Silas Marner,* and *Adam Bede* under the name George Eliot. Perhaps the most famous example involved the three Brontë sisters: Anne, Charlotte, and Emily. They used the names of Acton, Currer, and Ellis Bell, respectively.

The sisters were three of six children born to Maria and Patrick Brontë. Their mother died when the oldest child was just seven, and their father, a country parson, raised his children with the help of their aunt. The two oldest girls soon died of tuberculosis, a disease that would figure heavily in the family's history.

Anne, Charlotte, and Emily eventually moved back in with their father and published a book of poetry in 1846. It sold only two copies. Emily's novel *Wuthering Heights* and Charlotte's novel *Jane Eyre* were both published the following year. They are considered among the greatest novels ever written and both have been made into movies several times. Anne wrote two novels, but neither was very successful.

Tragedy struck soon afterward. Branwell, the only male sibling in the family, died of tuberculosis in 1848. Emily caught cold at his funeral. It turned into tuberculosis and she died at the end of the year. Anne died of tuberculosis in 1849. Charlotte wrote two more novels but died—also of tuberculosis—in 1855.

As an indication of how highly *Jane Eyre* and *Wuthering Heights* are regarded, they are published today under their authors' real names.

But old habits die hard. When a young woman wrote a book about a youthful wizard several years ago, her publishing company asked her to use her initials instead of her actual name. They were afraid that boys wouldn't buy a book written by a woman.

They were wrong. Millions of boys—and girls—have purchased Harry Potter books written by Joanne Kathleen Rowling.

This portrait of Chopin at work was drawn by George Sand around 1847, shortly before their relationship came to an end. By this time he was very ill with tuberculosis.

Masters of

Music

CHAPTER

5

Alone

Not surprisingly, Chopin did not compose much music after his breakup with George Sand. He was too depressed. And he no longer had anyone to take care of him. He became even more ill. He often coughed up blood.

Because of his health, he had to cut back on lessons, which reduced his income. Even though he was not feeling well, his friends urged him to give a concert. That would help generate some money. Held in February 1848, the concert was a huge success. It quickly sold out and left a long waiting list. But it would be the final time that Chopin would perform in public in his adopted city.

Outside influences also intervened. The year 1848 was a historic one in Europe. All over the continent, people rose up against their rulers. France was no exception. There had been a bad harvest two years earlier. People were short of food. Many businesses failed, which threw thousands of people out of work. The government of King Louis-Philippe, which had been welcomed when it was established in 1830, proved to be corrupt. In February, the people revolted. Louis-Philippe had to choose between leaving France and staying, which would have plunged the country into a civil war. He left.

In all the chaos, people weren't interested in concerts. It could be dangerous to be outside at all. Taking music lessons wasn't worth the risk, either. Many of Chopin's students stayed away. His carefully ordered world started to fall apart.

Fortunately, a very wealthy English pupil of his named Jane Stirling invited him to visit her in London. He traveled there in April and became an immediate sensation. It seemed that everyone wanted to hear him play the piano. He performed in two public concerts and frequently for small gatherings, mainly in the homes of aristocrats. He even received an invitation from Queen Victoria.

He made enough money from these appearances to ease his financial worries. In addition, he was able to give lessons to a number of people who were willing to pay more for him than they would for most of the local tutors. He began to consider the possibility of making a new home in England.

But there were drawbacks as well. The air in London was similar to modern-day smog, which irritated Chopin's lungs. He grew even weaker. Sometimes his valet had to carry him to bed and undress him. Jane Stirling did her best to take care of him. She may even have been in love with him. If she was, it wouldn't have made any difference. Chopin wasn't interested in her. He was probably still trying to get over his feelings for George Sand. He didn't speak English, which made it hard for him to communicate. He missed his friends and their long, intimate conversations. Even if he had been able to speak the language, there were important cultural differences.

"These English are so different from the French, whom I have grown to accept as my own people," he wrote in a letter to his family. "They are kind people, but so weird."[1]

Part of what Chopin termed "weird" may have been their attitude toward music in general. He felt that they regarded it as something that plays quietly in the background while people do something else. For Chopin, music was life. It wasn't something to be treated almost with indifference.

As Tad Szulc writes, "He complained that English high society was surrounded by music from morning until night to the point where 'they do not care whether it is good or bad music. . . . They have a flower exhibit with music, dinner with music, charity functions with music.'" [2] There was also a personal element involved. Chopin felt that the English didn't really understand his music.

In the summer, it was common for well-to-do Londoners to leave the city for their summer homes. Many of these homes were in Scotland. Chopin had lots of invitations to visit these places, especially from friends and relatives of Jane's. But he wasn't any happier. He still could barely understand what people were saying, and many of the homes he visited were in remote locations.

When he returned to London in November, the skies were cold and gray. He felt even more isolated and wanted to return to his friends in Paris. He gave what would be his final public performance in the middle of the month. By then he was so weak that he could barely sit at the piano. A week later, he returned to Paris.

His friends were shocked at his appearance. He was obviously suffering from tuberculosis, the same disease that had claimed his sister Emilia. Making things even worse, the physician who had been treating him and to whom he gave the credit for keeping him alive this long had died not long before. The news may have seemed almost like a death sentence to the sick man.

But Chopin refused to give up. He began working on what would become his final compositions. He even tried to take on piano students. But he was too weak to continue with most of them for more than a few weeks. Because he had not composed anything for some time, he had little money. Fortunately, his friends gave him money. So did Jane Stirling.

Just as important, he spent a great deal of time with his friends. Solange was a frequent visitor. Another was Berlioz, who wrote of Chopin, "His weakness and his sufferings had become so great that he could no longer either play the piano or compose; even the slightest conversation fatigued him in an alarming manner. He endeavored generally to make himself understood as far as possible by signs."[3]

One of the few photographic images of Chopin dates from this time and clearly shows his suffering. His eyes show him in a great deal of pain, and his arms are crossed over his stomach as if that too is troubling him.

In late June, Chopin was so weak that he wrote a desperate appeal to the surviving members of his family, asking them to visit. His sister Louise arrived in early August. George Sand wrote to Louise a few weeks later, asking for news of his condition. There was still too much resentment. Louise ignored her.

But not even the presence of Louise and his friends could help him. He died early on the morning of October 17, 1849.

His funeral was held in Paris. At his request, Mozart's *Requiem* was played during the ceremonies. It was an appropriate choice. Like Chopin, who died at the age of 39, Mozart was also in his 30s when he died. Chopin's body was buried in Père-Lachaise Cemetery in Paris, along with a small urn containing Polish soil, which Chopin had always kept with him.

But one part of him was missing at the burial. Louise took his heart back to his beloved Warsaw with her. It remains to this day in the Church of the Holy Cross.

Digging for gold

THE
Forty-Niners

On January 24, 1848, John Marshall was supervising a work crew that was building a sawmill on California's American River for his boss, a man named John Sutter. Marshall happened to notice a glint in the shallow waters. He picked up a small piece of gold. Soon afterward, two other men found nuggets in nearby rivers.

That was the beginning of the California Gold Rush. When word got out, it ignited a frenzy of "gold fever." Thousands of people swarmed west in search of instant wealth. Because this migration began in 1849, these people were called 49ers. Getting to the gold fields wasn't easy. Since most of the population of the United States still lived east of the Mississippi River, there were three choices. One was a dangerous 15,000-mile voyage around Cape Horn at the tip of South America to San Francisco. The second was to sail to the east side of the isthmus of Panama, cross the jungle and mountains while risking tropical diseases, then catch another ship on the west side and complete the trip. Third was an overland journey of more than 2,000 miles.

The difficulties didn't matter. By some estimates, more than 300,000 people made the grueling trek in the first five years of the gold rush. San Francisco Bay became clogged with abandoned ships as their crews joined the hordes heading for the gold fields.

Once they arrived, there was no guarantee of success. Mining was hard work. It was also dangerous. In addition to accidents, there was a lot of crime. In fact, very few people found much gold. Many merchants became rich by selling food and other supplies to the miners. One of them was Levi Strauss, a German immigrant who is famous because he invented jeans.

An important result of the gold rush was that California, which the United States had acquired from Mexico in 1848, became a state in 1850. Reflecting the importance of John Marshall's sharp eyesight, its nickname is "The Golden State."

Selected Works

Virtually everything that Chopin composed was for the piano. These include:

Piano Concerto #1

Piano Concerto #2

Sonata in B Minor

Sonata for Piano and Cello

55 mazurkas

13 polonaises

24 preludes

27 études (studies)

19 nocturnes

four ballades

four scherzos

Chronology

1810   Born on March 1 in Zelazowa Wola, Poland

1816   Begins taking piano lessons from Albert Zywny

1818   Plays at charity concert in Warsaw

1822   Begins studying composition with Jósef Elsner

1826   Enters Warsaw Conservatory

1828   Visits Berlin

1829   Performs in Vienna to great acclaim

1830   Leaves Warsaw

1831   Arrives in Paris

1832   First concert appearance in Paris

1835   Meets parents in Karlsbad, Germany

1836   Proposes to Maria Wodzinska, meets George Sand

1837   Maria Wodzinska breaks off engagement

1838   Becomes romantically involved with George Sand; travels to Majorca with Sand and her children; they all return to Paris

1844   Father dies

1847   Ends relationship with George Sand

1848   From Paris, travels to England and Scotland

1849   Dies on October 17

1803 French composer Hector Berlioz is born.

1804 Napoléon Bonaparte declares himself emperor of France.

1809 German composer Felix Mendelssohn is born and Austrian composer Franz Joseph Haydn dies.

1810 The movement toward Mexican independence begins with "El Grito de Dolores."

1811 Hungarian composer Franz Liszt is born.

1815 Czar Alexander I of Russia declares that Poland is a part of Russia.

1819 Pianist Clara Schumann is born.

1821 Greek War of Independence begins; it ends in 1829 with Greek victory.

1827 Composer Ludwig van Beethoven dies.

1830 Louis-Philippe succeeds Charles X as king of France in July Revolution.

1833 German composer Johannes Brahms is born.

1837 Victoria becomes British Queen; her reign lasts until 1901.

1840 Russian composer Peter Tchaikovsky is born.

1843 Charles Dickens publishes *A Christmas Carol*.

1846 U.S.-Mexico War begins; ends two years later as United States acquires future states of Arizona, California, Nevada, New Mexico, Texas, Utah, and parts of Colorado and Wyoming.

1847 Emily Brontë publishes *Wuthering Heights,* and her sister Charlotte publishes *Jane Eyre*.

1848 Gold is discovered in California. French revolt against Louis-Philippe; other revolutions occur in Berlin, Vienna, Venice, Milan, Rome, and Warsaw.

1850 California is admitted to the United States.

1861 U.S. Civil War begins.

1862 Small Mexican army overcomes invading French troops on May 5.

1865 U.S. Civil War ends; president Abraham Lincoln is assassinated.

1896 Clara Schumann dies.

1918 Poland regains independence.

1939 German army invades Poland to start World War II.

1945 World War II ends with the defeat of Germany.

1990 Lech Walesa becomes the first postwar president of the Republic of Poland.

2002 Movie *The Pianist* is released and wins Academy Awards for Best Actor (Adrien Brody) and Best Director (Roman Polanski).

Chapter Notes

Chapter 1   The Patriotic Pianist
 [1] William Shirer, *The Rise and Fall of the Third Reich*, (New York: Simon and Schuster, 1960), p. 599.
 [2] "'The Pianist' Soundtrack Lands at Number One (With a Bullet) On Billboard's Classical Chart." PR Newswire, April 2, 2003, http://www.findarticles.com/cf_dls/m4PRN/2003_April_2/99511605/p1/article.jhtml.

Chapter 2   Growing Up Happy
 [1] George R. Marek and Maria Gordon-Smith, *Chopin*, (New York: Harper and Row, 1978), p. 9.
 [2] William G. Atwood, *Fryderyk Chopin: Pianist from Warsaw*, (New York: Columbia University Press, 1987), p. 2.
 [3] George R. Marek and Maria Gordon-Smith, *Chopin*, (New York: Harper and Row, 1978), p. 14.
 [4] Ibid., p. 15.
 [5] Ibid., p. 12.
 [6] William G. Atwood, *Fryderyk Chopin: Pianist from Warsaw*, (New York: Columbia University Press, 1987), p. 9.
 [7] George R. Marek and Maria Gordon-Smith, *Chopin*, (New York: Harper and Row, 1978), p. 15.
 [8] Ibid.
 [9] Ibid.

Chapter 3   On to Paris
 [1] Derek Melville, *Chopin*, (Hamden, CT: Linnet Books, 1977), p. 25.
 [2] Ibid., p. 29.
 [3] Ibid., p. 31.
 [4] http://azaz.essortment.com/robertclarasch_rjya.htm.

Chapter 4   George Sand
 [1] William G. Atwood, *Fryderyk Chopin: Pianist from Warsaw*, (New York: Columbia University Press, 1987), p. 115.
 [2] Adam Zamoyski, *Chopin: A New Biography*, (New York: Doubleday and Co., 1980), p. 172.
 [3] Derek Melville, *Chopin*, (Hamden, CT: Linnet Books, 1977), p. 36.
 [4] Ibid., p. 37.
 [5] Harold Schonberg, *The Lives of Great Composers*, (New York: W. W. Norton & Company, 1981), p. 192.
 [6] Julius H. Jacobson, *The Classical Music Experience* (Naperville, Ill.: Sourcebooks, Inc., 2003), p. 90.
 [7] Harold Schonberg, *The Lives of Great Composers*, (New York: W. W. Norton & Company, 1981), p. 192.

Chapter 5   Alone
 [1] Adam Zamoyski, *Chopin: A New Biography*, (New York: Doubleday and Co., 1980), p. 295.
 [2] Tad Szulc, *Chopin in Paris*, (New York: Scribner, 1998), p. 377.
 [3] Ibid., p. 391.

Glossary

aspic (AS-pick)—gelatin dish containing meat, vegetables, fruit, or a combination of ingredients

banalities (beh-NAH-luh-tees)—commonplace words with no emotional meaning

borscht (BORSHT)—beet soup served hot or cold, often with sour cream

compote (KOM-pote)—fruit stewed in syrup

concentration camp (con-sen-TRAY-shun KAMP)—prison in which inmates are kept under especially brutal conditions and are frequently put to death

concerto (con-CHAIR-toe)—musical composition for solo instrument and orchestra, usually in three movements

conservatory (con-SERVE-uh-tor-ee)—music school

czar (ZAHR)—ruler of Russia

exiles (ECK-ziles)—people who either have voluntarily left their native land or have been ordered to leave

hemorrhaged (HEM-ridged)—ruptured, causing excessive bleeding

improvise (IM-proe-vize)—to make up a musical composition on the spur of the moment without prior preparation

kulebiaka (koo-lee-BYAH-kuh)—Russian dish consisting of one or more ingredients inside a hot pastry shell

lapis lazuli (LAP-is LAH-zeh-lee)—a bright blue gemstone, often with gold-colored flecks

lyceum (lie-SEE-um)—a type of secondary school

mazurka (meh-ZUR-kuh)—lively Polish dance similar to a polka

nocturne (NOCK-turn)—slow, sentimental composition that reflects the calmness of the night

nom de plume (NAHM-dih-PLUHM)—French phrase that means "pen name"

polonaise (paul-uh-NASE)—a somewhat formal marchlike Polish dance, or the music written for such a dance

prelude (PRAY-lyood)—music designed to be played before other pieces; short piano piece

requiem (REH-kwee-em)—Catholic mass for someone who has just died; music performed for such a mass

scherzo (SKAIRT-zoe)—lively short piece of music

soiree (swah-RAY)—an elegant party held in the evening

sonata (seh-NAH-teh)—composition for piano or another instrument with piano accompaniment, usually in three or four movements

virtuoso (vir-choo-OH-so)—extremely skilled musician

For Further Reading

For Young Adults

Cencetti, Greta. *Chopin*. New York: McGraw Hill Consumer Products, 2001.

Eisler, Benita. *Chopin's Funeral*. New York: Knopf, 2003.

Patton, Barbara. *Introducing Frederic Chopin*. Soundboard Books, 1990.

Vernon, Roland. *Introducing Chopin*. Parsippany, NJ: Silver Burdett Press, 1996.

Works Consulted

Books

Atwood, William G. *Fryderyk Chopin: Pianist from Warsaw*. New York: Columbia University Press, 1987.

Huneker, James. *Chopin: The Man and His Music*. New York: Dover Publications, 1966.

Jacobson, Julius H. *The Classical Music Experience*. Naperville, Ill.: Sourcebooks, Inc., 2003.

Marek, George R., and Maria Gordon-Smith. *Chopin*. New York: Harper and Row, 1978.

Melville, Derek. *Chopin*. Hamden, Conn.: Linnet Books, 1977.

Orga, Ates. *Chopin: His Life and Times,* New York: Two Continents Publishing, 1978.

Reich, Susanna. *Clara Schumann: Piano Virtuoso*. New York: Clarion Books, 1999.

Schonberg, Harold. *The Lives of the Great Composers*. New York: W.W. Norton & Company, 1981.

Shirer, William. *The Rise and Fall of the Third Reich*. New York: Simon and Schuster, 1960.

Szulc, Tad. *Chopin in Paris*. New York: A Lisa Drew Book/Scribner, 1998.

Zamoyski, Adam. *Chopin: A New Biography*. New York: Doubleday and Company, 1980.

For Serious Researchers

Much of Chopin's life has been pieced together from original nineteenth-century documents like letters, music manuscripts, and concert programs, articles and reviews in newspapers and magazines, and drawings and paintings of Chopin by people who knew him. Much of it has survived time, some of it has been translated into English, and there are bits and pieces of his life reposited around the world. One institution that holds a great deal of material on Chopin's life in Paris is the Société Historique et Littéraire Polonaise in Paris, France.

On the Internet

Frédéric Chopin

http://www.classicalarchives.com/chopin.html

http://www.chopin.org

http://www.chopin.pl

http://www.polamjournal.com/Library/Biographies/Chopin/chopin.html

"'The Pianist' Soundtrack Lands at Number One (With a Bullet) On Billboard's Classical Chart." <u>PR Newswire</u>, April 2, 2003 http://www.findarticles.com/cf_dls/m4PRN/2003_April_2/99511605/p1/article.jhtml

A Brief History of Poland

http://www.polandonline.com/history.html

http://www.polandcarolina.org/History/BriefPolishHistory.htm

Mexico's "Fourth of July"

http://www.sanmiguelguide.com/tour-el-grito.htm

http://www.onwar.com/aced/data/mike/mexico1810b.htm

http://www.go2mexico.com/?page=mexico_articles/el_grito.php

Clara Schumann

http://www.geneva.edu/-dksmith/clara/schumann.html

http://azaz.essortment.com/robertclarasch_rjya.htm

Women Take Pen Names

http://www.btinternet.com/-i.c.palmer/brontes.htm

http://www.geocities.com/mebirmingham/history.htm

The Forty-Niners

http://www.calgoldrush.com/

http://ceres.ca.gov/ceres/calweb/geology/goldrush.html

Index